MY MONEY

MY MIND

Teachings on the Behavior and Tools in the Psychology of Wealth

JESSICA GERALD

MY MONEY MY MIND

Copyright © 2023 Jessica Gerald

Print in USA

For authorization requests, write to the publisher below:

Jessica Gerald

pooly_promise@yahoo.com

DEDICATION

To all persons seeking a better life

OTHER BOOKS FROM AUTHOR:

Inner Life with Pets: Dream Messages from the Afterlife

The "I" Fasting Woman: 15 Recipes for Cyclic Intermittent Fasting for Women with Shorter Menstrual Cycles

Sober Up Bitch: Transform Into An Alcohol Free Woman

Table of Content

INTRODUCTION

Do you find yourself making impulsive spending decisions that you later regret? Do you struggle to stick to a budget? Do you worry about running out of money?

If so, you're not alone. Many people struggle with their relationship with money. But what if I told you that there is a way to change your relationship with money and achieve financial freedom?

In my book, **My Money My Mind**, I will teach you the psychology of wealth. I will show you how your thoughts, beliefs, and behaviors about money are holding you back from achieving your financial goals.

I will also teach you the tools you need to change your relationship with money. You will learn how to set financial goals, create a budget, and stick to it. You will also learn how to invest your money wisely and build wealth over time.

My Money My Mind is more than just a book about money. It is a book about changing your life. If you are ready to take control of your finances and achieve financial freedom, then this book is for you.

If you are interested in learning more about the psychology of wealth, then I encourage you to check out the book. We would love to hear from you on how this book has helped you.

UNRAVELING THE MONEY MINDSET

Our money mindset is the foundation of our financial well-being. It is the set of beliefs, attitudes, and emotions that we have about money. Our money mindset influences how we earn, spend, save, and invest our money.

If we have a healthy money mindset, we are more likely to be financially successful. We are more likely to set and achieve financial goals, and we are less likely to experience financial stress.

However, if we have a negative money mindset, we are more likely to struggle financially. We may be more likely to make impulsive spending decisions, and we may be more likely to experience anxiety or fear about money.

Our money mindset is shaped by our upbringing, our experiences, and the messages we receive from the media and society. If we grew up in a household where money was scarce, we may have learned that money is scarce and that we should be afraid of it. If we experienced financial hardship, we may have learned that money is unreliable and that we can't rely on it.

The good news is that our money mindset is not set in stone. We can change our money mindset by challenging our limiting beliefs about money and by practicing new behaviors.

Limiting Beliefs about Wealth

One of the most important things we can do to improve our money mindset is to identify and challenge our limiting beliefs about wealth. Limiting beliefs are negative beliefs. These are beliefs that we hold about ourselves and our abilities. They can hold us back from achieving our goals, including our financial goals.

Some common limiting beliefs about wealth include:

* I'm not good with money.

* I'll never be rich.

* Rich people are greedy and selfish.

* I don't deserve to be wealthy.

These beliefs are often based on our experiences, our upbringing, and the messages we receive from the media and society. However, they are not true. They are simply limiting beliefs that we have learned to believe.

How to Challenge Limiting Beliefs

Once we have identified what our limiting beliefs are, we can start to make effort to challenge them. Here are some tips for challenging limiting beliefs:

Question the belief.

Ask yourself where you learned the belief and why you believe it. Is there any evidence to support the belief?

Find evidence to refute the belief

Look for examples of people who have overcome their limiting beliefs about wealth.

Replace the belief with a positive belief

What would you rather believe about yourself and your ability to achieve wealth?

Take action

Start taking steps to achieve your financial goals. This will help you to see that you are capable of achieving wealth.

Exercise: Identifying and Challenging Limiting Beliefs

Here is an exercise to help you identify and challenge your limiting beliefs about wealth:

1. Take a few minutes to write down all of the beliefs you have about wealth.

2. Next to each belief, write down why you believe it.

3. Now, ask yourself if there is any evidence to support the belief. If not, challenge the belief.

4. Replace the belief with a positive belief.

5. Finally, take action to start living in accordance with your new belief.

....

....

....

CHAPTER TWO

THE PSYCHOLOGY OF SPENDING

Our spending habits are influenced by a variety of factors, including our emotions, values, and social environment. These factors can lead us to make impulsive purchases, overspend, or even fall into debt.

Emotions

One of the most powerful drivers of our spending habits is our emotions. When we're feeling happy, excited, or stressed, we're more likely to make impulsive purchases. This is because our emotions can cloud our judgment and make us less likely to think about the long-term consequences of our spending.

For example, if you're feeling stressed after a long day at work, you might be more likely to go out to eat or buy something from a vending machine. Even though you know these purchases aren't the best use of your money, you might do it anyway because it's a way to feel better in the moment.

Values

Our values also play a role in our spending habits. If we value possessions, we're more likely to spend money on material goods. If we value experiences, we're more likely to spend money on travel, entertainment, or other activities.

For example, if you value possessions, you might be more likely to buy a new car or a new piece of furniture even if you don't really need it. If you value experiences, you might be more likely to take a vacation or go out to eat with friends.

Social Environment

The social environment we live in can also influence our spending habits. If we're surrounded by people who spend a lot of money, we're more likely to do the same. This is because we want to fit in and be seen as successful.

For example, if your friends are always going out to expensive restaurants, you might feel pressure to do the same. Even though you know you can't afford it, you might do it anyway because you don't want to be left out.

How to Develop a Mindful Spending Approach

If you're struggling with your spending habits, there are a few things you can do to develop a more mindful approach to spending.

- Be aware of your emotions.

When you're about to make a purchase, ask yourself how you're feeling. Are you feeling happy, excited, stressed, or something else? Once you're aware of your emotions, you can start to think about whether or not the purchase is really a good idea.

- Consider your values.

What are the things that are most important to you? Are you spending your money on things that align with your values? If not, you might want to reconsider your purchases.

- Think about the long-term consequences.

When you're about to make a purchase always think about the long-term consequences. Will this purchase help you reach your financial goals? Or will it set you back?

- Set a budget and stick to it.

A budget can help you track your spending and stay on track. Once you have a budget, make sure you stick to it. This will help you avoid overspending.

- Be patient.

It takes time to develop a mindful spending approach. Don't get discouraged if you slip up along the way. Just keep at it and you'll soon get there.

By understanding the factors that influence our spending habits, we can start to develop a more mindful approach to spending. This can help us avoid overspending, reach our financial goals, and live a more fulfilling life.

CHAPTER THREE

EMBRACING A SAVING AND INVESTING MINDSET

There are many psychological barriers that can prevent people from saving and investing. Some of these barriers include:

- Fear of loss.

Many people are afraid of losing money, so they avoid investing altogether. This fear can be especially strong for people who have experienced financial hardship in the past.

- Procrastination.

It can be easy to put off saving and investing, especially when there are other more immediate financial demands. However, the longer you wait to start saving, the more difficult it will be to reach your financial goals.

- Lack of knowledge.

Many people simply don't know how to save and invest effectively. This can lead to them making poor financial decisions that can cost them money in the long run.

Tools and Techniques for Building a Successful Savings and Investment Plan

There are a number of tools and techniques that can help you build a successful savings and investment plan. These include:

- Creating a budget.

A budget is a great way to track your income and expenses, and identify areas where you can cut back in order to free up more money to save and invest.

- Setting financial goals.

Once you know how much money you have to work with, you can start setting financial goals. These goals can be short-term, such as a down payment for a house, or a long-term one, such as saving up for retirement.

- Automating your savings.

One of the best ways to make sure you're saving money on a regular basis is to automate your savings. This can mean setting up a direct deposit from your salary into your savings account.

- Investing for the long term.

The best way to grow your money over time is to invest it. However, it is very important to note that investing carries some risk. Therefore, it's important to invest for the long term so that you have time to ride out any short-term fluctuations in the market.

How One Person Transformed Their Savings Habit

John Sellar was always a spender. He earned a good amount in the I.T industry. He never seemed to have any money saved, and he was always living paycheck to paycheck. One day, John decided that he had had enough. He was tired of being broke, and he wanted to start building a better financial future for himself.

John started by creating a budget. He tracked his income and expenses, and identified areas where he could cut back. He also set some financial goals, such as saving for a down payment on a house.

John then automated his savings. He set up a direct deposit from his paycheck into his savings account. This way, he didn't have to think about saving money; it just happened automatically.

John also started investing his money. He invested in a diversified portfolio of stocks and bonds. He knew that investing carried some risk, but he was willing to take that risk in order to grow his money over the long term.

Over time, John's savings habits transformed. He started saving more money, and he invested his money wisely. As a result, his financial situation improved dramatically. He was able to buy a house, and he started saving for retirement.

John's story is a reminder that anyone can transform their savings habits. It takes a lot of hard work and dedication to achieve, but it's possible. If you're ready to start saving and investing, there are a number of tools and techniques that can help you reach your financial goals.

A saving and investing mindset is essential for achieving financial success. By overcoming the psychological barriers to saving and investing, and by using the right tools and techniques, you can build a successful savings and investment plan that will help you achieve your financial goals.

CHAPTERFOUR

OVERCOMING FINANCIAL FEARS AND ANXIETY

Financial fears and anxiety are common experiences. They can be caused by a number of factors that includes:

- Past financial experiences.

If you have had negative financial experiences in the past, such as bankruptcy or job loss, you may be more likely to experience financial anxiety.

- Current financial situation.

If you are struggling to make ends meet, you may be more likely to experience financial anxiety.

- Cultural factors.

Some cultures place a high value on financial security, which can lead to increased financial anxiety.

Financial fears and anxiety can manifest in a number of ways, including:

- Worrying about money.

This can be a constant and overwhelming fear.

- Avoidance of financial tasks.

This can include things like paying bills, balancing a budget, or investing.

- Irritability and anger.

This can be caused by the stress of financial worries.

- Physical symptoms.

This can include headaches, stomachaches, and insomnia.

If you are experiencing financial fears and anxiety, there are a number of things you can do to overcome them.

Mindful practices

Mindful practices can help you to become more aware of your thoughts and feelings about money. This can help you to challenge negative thoughts and beliefs about money, and to develop a more positive relationship with money.

Some mindful practices that can help you to overcome financial fears and anxiety include:

Meditation: Meditation can help you to focus on the present moment and to let go of negative thoughts and feelings.

Yoga: Yoga can help you to relax and to reduce stress.

Journaling - Journaling can help you to explore your thoughts and feelings about money.

Common fears and anxiety related to money

Some of the most common fears and anxiety related to money include:

- Fear of debt.

This is the fear of being in debt, and of the consequences of not being able to repay debt.

- Fear of not being able to afford basic necessities.

This is the fear of not being able to afford food, shelter, or other essential items.

- Fear of not being able to retire comfortably.

This is the fear of not having enough money to live comfortably in retirement.

How one person conquered their financial fears....

Sarah Letright was always worried about money. She grew up in a poor family, and she had seen firsthand the financial struggles that her parents had faced. As a result, Sarah was always afraid of not having enough money. She had been working for years as a teacher and was living by quite okay, or so she thought.

Sarah's fear of money led her to make some poor financial decisions. She would often overspend, and she would avoid saving money. She was also afraid to invest, because she was afraid of losing money.

Sarah's financial fears were holding her back from living her life to the fullest. She was constantly stressed about money, and she was afraid to take risks.

One day, Sarah decided to change. She was tired of being afraid of money, and she wanted to start living a more financially secure life.

Sarah started by learning more about money. She read books, took financial courses, and talked to a financial advisor. She also started tracking her income and expenses, and she created a budget.

As Sarah learned more about money, she started to feel more confident in her ability to manage her finances. She also started to make better financial decisions. She started saving money, and she started investing.

Over time, Sarah's financial fears started to dissipate. She was no longer afraid of not having enough money, and she was no longer afraid to take risks. She was finally able to live her life to the fullest, without worrying about money.

Sarah's story is a reminder that anyone can overcome their financial fears. If you're struggling with financial fears, there are resources available to help you. You can talk to a financial advisor, read books, or take financial courses. With hard work and dedication, you can overcome your financial fears and start living a more financially secure life.

CHAPTER FIVE

THE POWER OF GOAL SETTING AND VISUALIZATION

Goal setting and visualization are two powerful tools that can help you achieve your dreams. Goal setting gives you a clear target to aim for, while visualization helps you see yourself achieving your goal, which can boost your motivation and confidence.

When you set a goal, it's important to make sure it's specific, measurable, achievable, relevant, and time-bound (SMART). This will help you stay on track and make progress towards your goal.

Visualization is a mental exercise that involves imagining yourself achieving your goal. You can visualize yourself taking the steps necessary to reach your goal, or you can visualize the end result. The more detailed your visualization is, the more effective it will turn out to be.

There are many benefits to using goal setting and visualization together. For example, goal setting can help you:

* Stay motivated and focused

* Break down big goals into small manageable tasks

* Keep up with your progress and celebrate your successes, big or small.

Visualization can help you:

* See yourself achieving your goal, which can boost your confidence

* Identify any obstacles that may be preventing you from achieving your goal

* Develop a very good plan to overcome those obstacles

Here are some step-by-step instructions on how to set SMART financial goals:

1. Define your goal.

What do you want to achieve financially? Do you want to save for a down payment on a house or retire early?

2. Make your goal specific.

What is the exact amount of money you want to save or the date you want to retire by?

3. Make your goal measurable.

How will you track your progress towards your goal?

4. Make your goal achievable.

Is your goal realistic and within your reach?

5. Make your goal relevant.

 Is your goal aligned with your overall financial goals?

6. Make your goal time-bound.

By when do you want to achieve your goal?

Once you've defined your goal, you can start to visualize yourself achieving it. Close your eyes and imagine yourself saving for your down payment, paying off your debt, or retiring early. See yourself taking the steps necessary to reach your goal, and feel the excitement and satisfaction of achieving it.

Visualization can be a powerful tool to help you achieve your financial goals. By following these steps, you can set SMART financial goals and start visualizing your success today.

Here are some additional tips for using goal setting and visualization to achieve your financial goals:

* Reward yourself for your successes.

This will help you to stay positive and motivated.

* Don't give up! It's worth it in the end.

CHAPTER SIX

MASTERING THE ART OF NEGOTIATION

Negotiation is the skill of reaching an agreement between two or more parties on a subject matter. It is a skill that can be used in a variety of contexts, including personal finance.

In personal finance, negotiation can be used to secure better deals on a variety of things, such as:

Credit cards:

You can negotiate a lower interest rate or annual fee on your credit card.

Mortgages:

You can negotiate a lower interest rate or closing costs on your mortgage.

Car loans:

You can negotiate a lower interest rate or monthly payment on your car loan.

Insurance:

You can negotiate lower premiums on your car insurance, health insurance, or home insurance.

Debt consolidation:

You can negotiate a lower interest rate on your debt consolidation loan.

There are a number of negotiation strategies that can be used to secure better deals. Some of these strategies include:

Do your research:

Before you start negotiating, it is important to do your research and know your options. This will give you a better understanding of your bargaining power and what you are willing to accept.

Be prepared to walk away:

If you are not happy with the terms of the negotiation, be prepared to walk away. Walking away will show the other party that you are serious about getting a good deal.

Be assertive but not aggressive:

It is important to be assertive in negotiations, but not aggressive. This means being clear about your needs and wants, but not being rude or threatening.

Listen to the other party:

It is also important to listen to the other party in a negotiation. This will help you understand their needs and wants, and it may also give you some ideas for how to reach a mutually beneficial agreement.

Negotiation is a skill that one can learn and develop with time. By following these strategies, you can improve your chances of securing better deals in your personal finances.

Here are some additional tips for mastering the art of negotiation:

* Be confident. Believe in yourself and your ability to reach a good deal.

* Be prepared. Do all the research you can to know your options.

* Be flexible. Be willing to compromise and meet in the middle.

* Be respectful. Treat the other party with respect, even if you disagree with them.

* Be persistent. Don't give up until you reach an agreement that you are happy with.

Negotiation can be a powerful tool for improving your personal finances. By following these tips, you can master the art of negotiation and secure better deals on a variety of things.

Here are some examples of how negotiation can be used in personal finance:

- You are buying a car.

You can negotiate the price of the car, the interest rate on the loan, and the trade-in value of your current car.

- You are buying a house.

You can negotiate the purchase price of the house, the closing costs, and the terms of the mortgage.

- You are getting a job.

You can negotiate your salary, benefits, and vacation time.

- You are starting a business.

You can negotiate the terms of contracts with vendors, employees, and clients.

CHAPTER SEVEN

BUILDING RESILIENCE AND FINANCIAL CONFIDENCE

Financial resilience is the ability to stand financial shocks and setbacks without losing yourself. It is a key component of financial well-being, and it can be built by developing financial confidence and self-assurance.

Financial Confidence

Financial confidence is the belief in your ability to manage your finances effectively. It is having the knowledge, skills, and resources you need to make sound financial decisions and achieve your financial goals.

Self-Assurance

Self-assurance is the belief in your own worth and abilities. It is having the confidence to take risks, try new things, and overcome challenges.

Tips for Building Financial Confidence and Self-Assurance

- Get educated about personal finance.

The more you know about personal finance, the more confident you will feel about managing your money. There are many resources available to help you learn about personal finance, such as books, websites, and financial workshops.

- Set financial goals.

Having specific financial goals will give you something to work towards and help you stay motivated. Your goals should be realistic and achievable, and they should be tailored to your individual needs and circumstances.

- Work with a budget.

A budget is a plan for how you will spend your money. It will help you track your income and expenses, and it will help you make sure that you are not spending more money than you earn.

- Live below your means.

This means spending less money than you earn. It is a key part of building financial security and resilience.

- Save money.

Saving money is important for building financial security. It will give you a cushion in case of unexpected expenses, and it will help you reach your financial goals sooner.

- Invest your money.

Investing your money is a way to grow your wealth over time. There are many different investment options available, so you can choose one that is right for you.

- Get help from a financial advisor.

If you need help building financial confidence and self-assurance, a financial advisor can help you develop a plan and track your progress.

Building financial resilience and confidence takes time and effort, but it is worth it. When you are financially confident, you are better able to weather financial storms and achieve your financial goals. You are also more likely to make sound financial decisions that will benefit you in the long run.

The 7 C's of Resilience

In addition to the tips above, there are a few other things you can do to build resilience and financial confidence. These are the 7 C's of resilience:

* *Competence:* This means having the knowledge and skills you need to manage your finances effectively.

* *Confidence:* This means believing in your ability to make sound financial decisions.

* *Connection:* This means having a strong support network of family, friends, and financial professionals.

* *Character:* This means having the strength and determination to overcome financial challenges.

* *Contribution:* This means giving back to your community and making a difference in the world.

* *Coping:* This means having healthy coping mechanisms for dealing with financial stress.

* *Control:* This means feeling like you have some control over your financial future.

By focusing on this 7 C's, you can build the resilience and financial confidence you need to achieve your financial goals.

CHAPTER EIGHT

UNDERSTANDING THE IMPACT OF INSTANT GRATIFICATION

Instant gratification is the desire to have something immediately, without having to wait or delay gratification. It is a powerful force that can lead to impulsive spending, debt, and financial problems.

There are a number of reasons why instant gratification is so alluring. First, it feels good. When we get something we want right away, our brains release dopamine, a neurotransmitter that is associated with pleasure. This gives us a short-term boost of happiness.

Second, instant gratification is easy. It doesn't require any effort or planning. We can just go out and buy something, or click a button to order something online. This makes it very tempting to give in to our impulses.

Third, instant gratification is often seen as a sign of success. In our society, we are constantly bombarded with messages that tell us that we should have everything we want, and we should have it right now. This can make it seem like instant gratification is the only way to be happy.

The Adverse Effects of Instant Gratification on Wealth Building

Instant gratification can have a number of adverse effects on wealth building. First, it can lead to impulsive spending. When we give in to our impulses, we often end up spending money on things that we don't really need. This can quickly add up and lead to debt.

Second, instant gratification can make it difficult to save money. When we're always looking for the next quick fix, it's hard to put money away for the future. This can make it difficult to reach our financial goals, such as retirement or a down payment on a house.

Third, instant gratification can lead to poor financial decisions. When we're not thinking about the long-term consequences of our actions, we're more likely to make bad financial decisions. This can lead to problems such as overspending, debt, and bankruptcy.

In the journey we have embarked upon throughout this book, we have delved deep into the intricate web of behaviors and tools that shape the psychology of wealth. As we arrive at the final chapter, we find ourselves standing at the threshold of a profound realization - that wealth is not just a measure of monetary abundance, but a reflection of our thoughts, actions, and perspectives.

Throughout these pages, we have explored how our beliefs about money, success, and abundance can either propel us towards prosperity or shackle us in scarcity. We have dissected the habits of successful individuals, unveiling the secrets of disciplined saving, strategic investing, and calculated risk-taking. We have scrutinized the psychological biases that often lead us astray, causing us to make irrational financial decisions.

But beyond the mechanics of financial management, we have discovered that the true essence of wealth lies in the transformation of our mindset. We have witnessed the power of gratitude, humility, and generosity in creating a ripple effect that not only enriches our lives but uplifts those around us. We have learned that authentic connections and meaningful experiences are the true measures of wealth, far surpassing material possessions.

As we draw this journey to a close, it becomes evident that the psychology of wealth is not a destination, but an ongoing evolution. It is a continuous quest to align our thoughts and actions with our aspirations, to find harmony between our ambitions and our values. It is a call to cultivate self-awareness, to challenge our preconceptions, and to embrace discomfort as a catalyst for growth.

In the grand tapestry of life, wealth is but one thread, intricately woven with countless others - relationships, purpose, health, and fulfillment. As we bid farewell to this exploration, let us carry forth the lessons we have unearthed, the tools we have sharpened, and the wisdom we have acquired. Let us embark on our personal journeys armed with a newfound understanding of wealth, a deep appreciation for its multi-dimensional nature, and an unwavering commitment to harness its potential for the greater good.

May the pages of this book be a reminder that wealth is not merely a destination, but a dynamic voyage that invites us to navigate with intention, purpose, and compassion. As we turn the final page, let us step boldly into the realm of possibility, with hearts full of gratitude and minds open to the boundless opportunities that await.

The end of one chapter marks the beginning of another, and so, dear reader, I invite you to embrace your journey towards a wealthier, more enriched existence - a journey that starts within and extends far beyond the reaches of our wildest dreams.